T0322131

DAVID ATTENBOROUGH
Lines to Live By

POP PRESS

Pop Press, an imprint of Ebury Publishing
20 Vauxhall Bridge Road
London SW1V 2SA

Pop Press is part of the Penguin Random House group of companies
whose addresses can be found at global.penguinrandomhouse.com

First published by Pop Press in 2024

www.penguin.co.uk

A CIP catalogue record for this book is available from the British Library

ISBN: 9781529933345

Typeset in 10.5/14pt Optima Nova LT Pro by Jouve (UK), Milton Keynes
Printed and bound in Great Britain by Clays Ltd, Elcograf S.p.A.

The authorised representative in the EEA is Penguin Random House
Ireland, Morrison Chambers, 32 Nassau Street, Dublin D02 YH68

CONTENTS

Introduction

Activist, presenter, national treasure, and one of the world's most trusted voices, Sir David Attenborough has been educating us about planet earth for 70 years.

Sir David has taken us into remote jungles and rainforests, deep into the oceans, and across frozen, polar landscapes. Through him, we met baby gorillas, talented birds, inquisitive meerkats, protective penguins, and escapologist lizards. Sir David has also taken us back in time to see dinosaurs, and into the future, to contemplate the fate of our beautiful planet, and our very existence.

Known for his calm, soothing presence, Sir David's words, however, also pack a punch. He doesn't shy away from telling us how we each have a responsibility to look after planet earth.

David Attenborough Lines to Live By

A fierce advocate for protecting the environment, Sir David has spoken up about climate change, and the damage humans are doing. In this book, we share with you some of his most powerful phrases, from the positive and delighted, to the stark warnings for humans to take action.

Sir David's impact has been diverse, to say the least. He has had a ship named after him, and has appeared on a cover of The Beatles' Sgt. Pepper's Lonely Hearts Club Band album. Butterflies, spiders, lizards, and frogs have been named after him. Sir David has worked with presidents and royalty, and gave a rousing speech at COP 26, calling for humans to make changes. Winner of numerous awards, in 2022, The United Nations named him a 'Champion of the Earth'. That sums him up, really.

Yet, despite the challenges facing the planet, Sir David is also the first to share how awe-inspiring earth is. In this book, you will find many quotes that will leave you feeling more positive and hopeful about our collective future. So, read on to get motivated!

Climate
Change

'It is, surely, our responsibility to do everything within our power to create a planet that provides a home not just for us, but for all life on Earth.'

'Global warming and
the rise of the sea
temperatures is a
global phenomenon
which we're all
responsible for.'

'In my lifetime, I've witnessed a terrible decline. In yours, you could and should witness a wonderful recovery.'

'The natural world is
changing. It is the most
precious thing we
have and we need
to defend it.'

'Every one of us, no matter who we are or where we live, can and must play a part in restoring nature.'

'It's easy to feel overwhelmed or powerless by the scale of the issues facing our planet, but we have the solutions.'

'We have one final chance to create the perfect home for ourselves and restore the wonderful world we inherited.'

'What we do in the next few years will determine the next few thousand years.'

'Our planet is headed
for disaster.'

'My generation failed.
We've allowed it
to happen.'

Animals

'We are the most
inquisitive and
inventive of all animals.'

'Animals aren't
aggressive to you
unless you interfere
with them.'

'If there were ever a possibility of escaping the human condition and living imaginatively in another creature's world, it must be with the gorilla.'

'If I encountered a king cobra in the wild, I would be very alarmed.'

'I'm not over-fond of animals. I am merely astounded by them.'

'Animals, including ourselves, endure all kinds of hardships and overcome all kinds of difficulties.'

'Families have quarrels.'

'We're replacing the wild with the tame.'

'I'm particularly fond
of chameleons.'

'It is not difficult to discover an unknown animal.'

'If you are not careful,
you can be bitten by a
hundred different kinds
of mosquito.'

'Flatworms are very simple creatures.'

'Leopards have always been rare, but now conflict with people is causing their numbers to decline further.'

Pollution

'Anyone who thinks that you can have infinite growth in a finite environment is either a madman or an economist.'

'We depend on the natural world for all the food we eat, for the very air we breathe.'

'The Garden of Eden is
no more.'

'If we damage the natural world, we damage ourselves.'

'We must tackle this flood [of pollution] at the source.'

'Eight million tonnes of plastic ends up in our oceans, every year.'

'Hundreds of thousands
of people who are
doing the same thing,
that really does have
an effect.'

Birds

'You ever been chased
by an ostrich?'

'As long as there is light,
the skies belong not
to the mammals but
to birds.'

'Dragonflies may zig-zag and dodge but they are lucky to escape if the bird gets anywhere near them.'

'[Hummingbirds are]
the celebrities, the
stars, of the bird world.'

'[The Griffon Vultures
are] flying for fun!'

'Rosella parents are scrupulously fair.'

Protecting
Habitats

'Forests are dynamic
and resilient and can
rise from the ashes, if
we let them.'

'We have felled forests, drained swamps, and covered fertile meadows with concrete in order to build our homes and factories, airports and motorways.'

'The tragedy of our time has been happening all around us, barely noticeable from day to day – the loss of our planet's wild places, its biodiversity.'

'It is that range of biodiversity that we must care for – the whole thing – rather than just one or two stars.'

'Look after the natural world. It's the most precious thing we have.'

'From every region of the world there are stories that reveal nature's resilience and show how restoration is possible.'

Sea Creatures

'It's a world of extraordinary beauty and complexity.'

– *on coral reefs*

'Frogs and toads today are most impressive singers.'

'Marvels beyond your imagining.'

'From killer whales to krill, all life here ultimately depends upon Antartica's sea ice.'

'Life and death, predator, prey, fighting it out in the seas, 200 millions years ago, just down there.'

'This fish has a brain capable of calculating the air speed, altitude, and trajectory of a bird.'

'A dive on a coral reef can leave you dazzled by the sheer number, variety, and beauty of the fish.'

Places

'Our stable, reliable
planet no longer exists.'

'The Artic is warming
twice as fast as
anywhere else on
our planet.'

'Deserts may appear to be barren and empty, but they are of crucial importance to life.'

'Why would I want to
go and live on the
moon?'

'The space for the other creatures with which we share the world has become more and more restricted.'

'The pictures of Earth taken on that Apollo mission made us see our own world anew.'

Memories

'I have to confess that I hadn't actually seen much television.'

'I have been in a Land Rover that was charged by a rhinoceros, and that was tiresome.'

'Because my face and
voice is associated with
it, I get all the credit.'

'All the drama's there,
you see, you don't
create it.'

'I've got a cellar full
of rock.'

'I'm swanning round the world looking at the most fabulously interesting things. Such good fortune.'

'I've never met a child
who is not interested in
natural history.'

'It never really occurred
to me to believe
in God.'

'Evolution is as solid a historical fact as you could conceive.'

'Nature is full of thrilling stories.'

'I looked for fossils as a kid, and I've never stopped, really.'

Endangered
Species

'We hunted them
to death.'

'You must now be the judge as to whether these varied and extraordinary histories are tragedies or triumphs.'

'All organisms are
ultimately concerned
to pass on their genes to
the next generation.'

'They are the trials that
we also face ourselves.'

'We're facing a crisis.
And one that
has consequences
for us all.'

'I don't think we are going to become extinct. We're very clever and extremely resourceful – and we will find ways of preserving ourselves, of that I'm sure.'

'We are alone in space.'

'Earth's survival is essential for ours.'

'The mechanisms that we have for destruction are so wholesale and so frightening that we can exterminate whole ecosystems without even noticing it.'

'There is . . . no reason
to suppose that our stay
here will be any more
permanent than that
of the dinosaurs.'

'Africa has more endangered animals than anywhere else.'

'The evidence is so
overwhelming, and the
consequences of
ignoring it are so
catastrophic, that I had
to say something.'

Sustainable Living

'Greed does not
actually lead to joy.'

'We are going to have to live more economically than we do. And we can do that and, I believe we will do it more happily, not less happily.'

'I can drive, but I've never driven. Never had a reason, never had a car.'

'[Humans are] the greatest problem solvers to have ever existed on Earth.'

'You will be among the next characters who can, if they wish, tell the most extraordinary story of all – how human beings in the twenty-first century came to their senses and started to protect Planet Earth.'

'Don't waste food.
Don't waste electricity.'

'The continued existence of life now rests in our hands.'

'As the problems are of
our making, so the
solutions can be
ours too.'

'Human beings have over-run the world.'

'We showed what plastic has done to the creatures that live in the ocean.'

'I am an ardent recycler.
I would like to think
that it works.'

'I don't put an electric
fire on if I don't need it.
I do put on a sweater.'

'If we shift away from eating meat and dairy, and more towards a plant-based diet, then the sun's energy goes directly into growing our food.'

Acknowledgements

Page 8 from BBC, 'Planet Earth II Episode 6', (Dir. Fredi Devas, 2016). Page 9 from ABC, 'Australian Story: Into Hot Water', (Dir. Rebecca Latham). Page 10 from BBC News 'COP26: David Attenborough says world is looking to leaders' (2021). Page 11 from WWF Australia, '10 best quotes from David Attenborough' (2021). Page 12 from The Guardian, 'David Attenborough says nature is in crisis but 'we have the solutions' (Hannah Devlin, 2023). Page 13 from The Guardian, 'David Attenborough says nature is in crisis but 'we have the solutions' (Hannah Devlin, 2023). Page 14 from 'A Life on our Planet', (David Attenborough, 2020). Page 15 from WWF International, 'A message to world leaders' (2019). Page 16 from Netflix, 'David Attenborough: A Life on our Planet' (Dir. Alastair Fothergill, 2020). Page 17 from The 60 Minutes Interview, 27 Sept 2020. Page 20 from 'Foreword, Our Planet' (David Attenborough, 2019). Page 21 from Bafta, 'Natural History with Sir David Attenborough' (Sandi Toksvig, 2018). Page 22 from BBC, 'Life on Earth: Life in the Trees' (1979). Page 23 from The Independent, 'Sir David Attenborough Interview' (Jenn Selby, 2015). Page 24 from Global Citizen, '10 of Sir David Attenborough's Best Quotes and Moments' (Sarah Hazlehurst, 2018). Page 25 from 'The Trials of Life' David Attenborough, (2022). Page 26 from 'Foreword, Dynasties' (David Attenborough, 2018). Page 27 from Netflix, 'David Attenborough: A Life on our Planet' (Dir. Alastair Fothergill, 2020). Page 28 from Friday Night with Jonathan Ross, June 2019. Page 29 from 'Life on Earth' (David Attenborough, 2018). Page 30

Acknowledgements

from 'Life on Earth' (David Attenborough, 2018). Page 31 from 'Life on Earth' (David Attenborough, 2018). Page 32 from Netflix, 'Our Planet, Deserts and Grasslands'(Adam Chapman, 2020). Page 36 from Mongabay, 'David Attenborough: someone who believes in infinite growth is 'either a madman or an economist'' (Mark Cardwell, 2013). Page 37 from 'Foreword, Planet Earth II (David Attenborough, 2016). Page 38 from Davos, 'Speech at the World Economic Forum' (2019). Page 39 from Davos, 'Speech at the World Economic Forum' (2019). Page 40 from Ellen MacArthur Foundation, 'Solving Plastic Pollution', (2020). Page 41 from BBC, 'Sir David Attenborough's plastic message' (2018). Page 42 from BBC, 'Sir David Attenborough's plastic message' (2018). Page 46 from The Jonathan Ross Show, 2 February 2013. Page 47 from from 'Life of Birds' (David Attenborough, 2023). Page 48 from 'Life of Birds' (David Attenborough, 2023). Page 49 from 'Hummingbirds: Jewelled messengers' (Dir. Paul Reddish, 2012). Page 50 from BBC Studios, 'David Attenborough flies among birds of prey' (2007). Page 51 from BBC Studios, 'Feeding wild baby birds' (2007). Page 54 from 'Foreword, Our Planet' (David Attenborough, 2019). Page 55 from 'Foreword, Seven Worlds, One Planet' (David Attenborough, 2019). Page 56 from 'A Life on our Planet', (David Attenborough, 2020). Page 57 from WWF Australia, '10 best quotes from David Attenborough' (2021). Page 58 from Still Watching Netflix, 'Sir David Attenborough Answers Questions From Famous Fans' (2020). Page 59 from Still Watching Netflix, 'Sir David Attenborough Answers Questions From Famous Fans' (2020). Page 62 from Still Watching Netflix, 'Sir David Attenborough Answers Questions From Famous Fans' (2020). Page 63 from 'Life on Earth' (David Attenborough, 2018). Page 64 from 'Foreword, Blue Planet II' (David Attenborough, 2018). Page 66 from 'Attenborough and the Sea Dragon' (Dir. Sally Thomson, 2018). Page 67 from Blue Planet II: Series 1, Episode 1 (Dir. James Honeyborne, 2017). Page

Acknowledgements

68 from The Hunt: Race Against Time (2015). Page 72 from WWF International, 'A Message to World Leaders' (2019). Page 73 from Our Planet: Frozen Worlds (Dir. Sophie Lanfear, 2019). Page 74 from Our Planet: From Deserts to Grasslands (Dir. Adam Chapman, 2019). Page 75 from The 60 Minutes Interview, 27 Sept 2020. Page 76 from 'Foreword, Planet Earth II' (David Attenborough, 2019). Page 77 from 'Foreword, Our Planet' (David Attenborough, 2019). Page 80 from Life on Air (David Attenborough, 2010). Page 81 from The Observer, 'David Attenborough' (Kate Kellaway, 2010). Page 82 from Bafta, 'Natural History with Sir David Attenborough' (Sandi Toksvig, 2018).Page 83 from Bafta, 'Natural History with Sir David Attenborough' (Sandi Toksvig, 2018). Page 84 from The 60 Minutes Interview, 27 Sept 2020. Page 85 from The Guardian, 'Sir David Attenborough Warns against large families and predicts things will only get worse' (James Meikle, 2013). Page 86 from BBC Earth 'President Barack Obama Meets Sir David Attenborough' (2015). Page 87 from The Telegraph, 'Sir David Attenborough questioned on faith, naturally' (Tim Walker, 2009). Page 88 from The Times, 'David Attenborough on Charles Darwin' (Damian Whitworth, 2009). Page 89 from 'Foreword, Our Planet' (David Attenborough, 2019). Page 90 from The Jonathan Ross Show, June 2021. Page 94 from 'Life on Earth' (David Attenborough, 2018). Page 95 from 'Foreword, Dynasties' (David Attenborough, 2018). Page 96 from 'The Trials of Life' David Attenborough (2022). Page 97 from 'The Trials of Life' David Attenborough (2022). Page 98 from Extinction The Facts (Dir. Serena Davies, 2020). Page 99 from The Guardian, 'Sir David Attenborough Warns against large families and predicts things will only get worse' (James Meikle, 2013). Page 100 from Living Planet (David Attenborough, 1984). Page 101 from 'Foreword, Blue Planet II' (David Attenborough, 2018). Page 102 from Davos, 'Speech at the World Economic Forum'

Acknowledgements

(2019). Page 103 from 'Life on Earth' (David Attenborough, 2018). Page 104 from Cheltenham Festival, 'David Attenborough interview at The Times and The Sunday Times Cheltenham Literature Festival 2018' (Emma Freud, 2018). Page 105 from Cheltenham Festival, 'David Attenborough interview at The Times and The Sunday Times Cheltenham Literature Festival 2018' (Emma Freud, 2018). Page 108 from BBC News, 'Attenborough: 'Curb excess capitalism' to save nature.' (2020). Page 109 from BBC News, 'COP26: David Attenborough says world is looking to leaders' (2021). Page 110 from BBC News, 'COP26: David Attenborough says world is looking to leaders' (2021). Page 111 from from 'Foreword, Our Planet' (David Attenborough, 2023). Page 112 from 'Foreword, Our Planet' (David Attenborough, 2023). Page 113 from Still Watching Netflix, 'Sir David Attenborough Answers Questions from Famous Fans' (2020). Page 114 from Living Planet (David Attenborough, 1984). Page 115 from 'Foreword, Our Planet' (David Attenborough, 2019). Page 116 from 'David Attenborough: A Life on our Planet' (Dir. Alastair Fothergill, 2020). Page 117 from BBC Earth, 'David Attenborough Presents Seven Worlds One Planet Live From Glastonbury' (2019). Page 118 from The Observer, 'David Attenborough' (Kate Kellaway, 2010). Page 119 from The Observer, 'David Attenborough' (Kate Kellaway, 2010). Page 120 from BBC, 'Sir David Attenborough suggests a way of making space for nature.' (2023).